A Kid's Guide to Martial Arts

KARATE

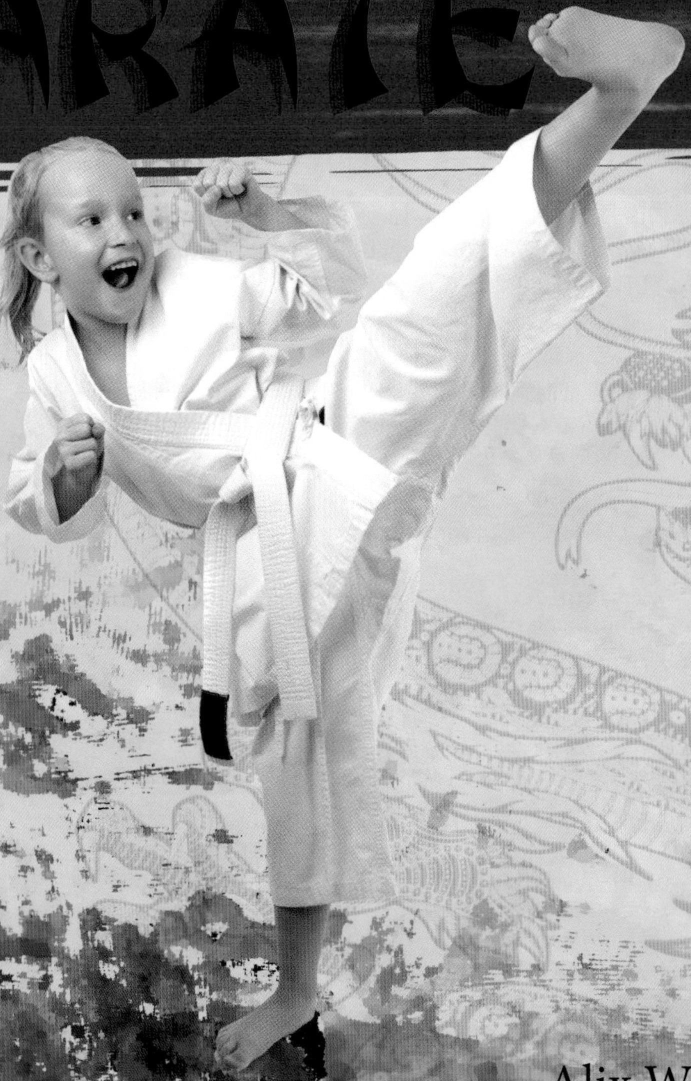

空手道

Alix Wood

PowerKiDS press
New York

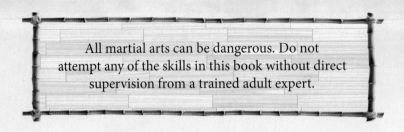

All martial arts can be dangerous. Do not attempt any of the skills in this book without direct supervision from a trained adult expert.

Published in 2013 by The Rosen Publishing Group, Inc.
29 East 21st Street, New York, NY 10010

Copyright © 2013 Alix Wood Books

Editor: Sara Antill
Designer: Alix Wood
Consultant: Sandra Beale-Ellis, National Association of Karate and Martial Art Schools (NAKMAS)

With grateful thanks to Finnian Cooling and everyone at Kernow Martial Arts; James, Joshua, and Elaine Latus, Olivia and Dereka Antonio, Solomon Brown, Ryan Fletcher, Alex Gobbitt, Hayden Hambly, Max Keeling, Joshua Nowell, Kyanna and Katie-Marie Orchard, Natasha Shear, Niamh Stephen, Chris Tanner, Jazmine Watkins, and Emily.

Photo Credits: Cover, 1, 4, 5, 7, 8, 9, 13 (bottom left), 15 (bottom left), 16 (bottom right), 17 (bottom right), 19 (bottom right) 20 (bottom left) 23 (top right & bottom right) 24 (bottom left), 26, 27, 28, 31 © Shutterstock; 6 © Gichin Funakoshi; all other images © Chris Robbins.

Library of Congress Cataloging-in-Publication Data

Wood, Alix.
  Karate / by Alix Wood.
     p. cm. — (A kid's guide to martial arts)
  Includes index.
  ISBN 978-1-4777-0314-4 (library binding) — ISBN 978-1-4777-0350-2 (pbk.) —
  ISBN 978-1-4777-0351-9 (6-pack)
  1. Karate—Juvenile literature. I. Title.
  GV1114.3.W68 2013
  796.815'3—dc23

                          2012020634

Manufactured in the United States of America

CPSIA Compliance Information: Batch #W13PK2: For Further Information contact Rosen Publishing, New York, New York at 1-800-237-9932

Contents

What Is Karate?

Karate is a martial art. Karate started on the Japanese island of Okinawa. The word "karate" means "empty hand." It is a type of fighting that uses no weapons.

In 1879 Okinawa came under Japanese rule. Many of the people of Okinawa didn't like this. To stop any fighting, Japan banned them from carrying weapons. The people began to secretly practice ways of fighting without weapons. They used martial arts they had seen from other parts of Asia. They called their style *te*. This was the start of present-day karate.

Map of Japan

JAPAN

Tokyo

Okinawa

Karate can be dangerous. It is very important to learn respect and self-control. At a karate school you may learn to **meditate**. To meditate you must close your eyes for a short time and prepare your thoughts. You will also learn how to bow, which shows respect to your teacher and your **opponent**. You can use karate to protect yourself. If you want to hurt people, you are studying karate for the wrong reason.

KARATEKA

People who do karate are called *karateka*. They use blocks, strikes, locks, and throws to beat their opponents.

This karateka is meditating with her eyes shut so she can concentrate on her breathing and think clearly.

Types of Karate

Many karate forms are developed from Shotokan. Shotokan was founded by Gichin Funakoshi (nicknamed Shoto), who was born in Okinawa in 1868. He set up a school of karate called "Shoto-kan," which means "club of Shoto."

Gichin Funakoshi believed karateka should be humble and gentle. Karateka must listen and take advice to improve. Manners are very important. Funakoshi believed many students would never use their karate skills in **combat**. He wanted his students to never be easily drawn into a fight. If students misuse what they have learned, they bring **dishonor** upon themselves.

Gichin Funakoshi

THE SHOTOKAN TIGER

This tiger is the symbol of Shotokan karate. The drawing was created by Funakoshi's friend and student, Hoan Kosugi. The symbol in the upper right hand corner is Hoan Kosugi's name.

Different Styles of Karate

Shotokan — deep **stances** and lunging movements

Kyokushin — full-contact, with punches, kicks, and board breaking

Wado-Ryu — combines jujitsu locks and throws with karate stances and strikes

Goju-Ryu — close-range fighting with grips

Isshin-Ryu — kicks, snappy punches with thumb-up fist, and blocking with the meaty part of the arm, not the bone

Shito-Ryu — develops dance-like forms

Uechi-Ryu — like Goju-Ryu, but strikes with fingertips or extended knuckles

Shorin-Ryu — like Shotokan, but more upright and uses more natural stances

Ice block breaking demonstration

Karate Equipment

*When doing karate, you wear a **gi**. This is a thin, white cotton jacket and pants with a belt tied around the waist.*

Put on the pants first. Some have a drawstring around the waist. Pull the string tight and then tie it through the loop at the front of the pants.

The jacket is tied by string at either side. The left side goes on top.

The belt is tied over the jacket at the waist. Girls ususally wear a white short sleeve T-shirt under the jacket. Boys do not wear the T-shirt.

Karate is done barefoot.

How to tie the belt

1 Place the middle of the belt on your stomach.

2 Pass each end of the belt behind you and back to the front.

3 Hold the belt together. Cross the right end over the left end, then thread it up behind both loops.

4 Cross the left end over the right end. Thread the left end back through the hole to finish the knot.

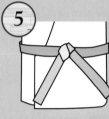

5 Both ends of the belt should be the same length and the ends should fall about halfway between your waist and knees.

THE BELT COLORS

Different clubs have different belt color order, but many follow this system. There are nine grades before you become a dan, or black belt.

White — beginner 9th kyu
Yellow — 8th kyu
Orange — 7th kyu
Green — 6th kyu
Blue — 5th kyu
Purple — 4th kyu
Brown — 3rd, 2nd, and 1st kyu
Black — 1st dan

"Kyu" means "nine" in Japanese.

The Dojo

*The **dojo** is the place where karateka learn their karate. Your dojo may be a multipurpose hall, or it may be a specially built martial arts dojo.*

The dojo is a special place and must be cared for by its users. The floor needs to be kept very clean, so you will not be allowed to enter the training area with shoes on. Some dojos have different doors for the instructors or the students to enter.

THE BOW

Stand up straight with your heels together and feet turned out slightly. Bend from the hips with your arms by your sides. Bow when you enter the dojo, and to your **sensei** as a sign of respect.

Many dojos will have a *shomen*.
A shomen is a display, typically
showing the name of the dojo, the
name of the style of martial art, and
perhaps an ornament or flowers.
They sometimes have a picture of
the founder of the style of karate,
with flags of Japan and the country
where the dojo is based.

A karate teacher is called a sensei.
Your sensei will help you learn karate
safely and in the correct way.

Warming Up

It is important to warm up before you start your karate session. Warming up stops you from pulling muscles. Try some of these exercises.

Remember, if you feel any pain, stop what you are doing and move onto a different exercise or stretch. Don't strain anything.

Arm swing

Stand with your feet shoulder width apart.

1

Twist your hips to the left and swing your arms.

2

Then turn to the right and swing your arms to the other side.

Neck stretches

Tip your head slowly forward, then back, then to the right, then to the left.

Side stretches

Stand with your feet placed shoulder width apart. Raise your left arm above your head and take a deep breath. Let your breath out slowly and lean to the right as far as possible. Then bend to the other side.

SAFETY

Do these simple things to make sure you don't hurt yourself or others when doing karate.

- Remove all jewelry and watches.
- Tie back long hair.
- Keep toenails and fingernails short.

Karate Stances

To be good at karate you need to learn how to stand. Stances give you balance and control. Different stances are useful for different moves.

"Dachi" means "stance." There are high, middle, and low height stances. Try making your feet match these stances. The red line going across is where your shoulders should be, over your feet.

High stance (*Musubi-dachi* or open toe stance)
Put your heels together, toes pointing out slightly. This stance is used to make a bow.

Low forward stance (*Zenkutsu-dachi*)
Lean your weight mostly on the front leg. Your rear leg should be very straight. Your front foot points forward. Your rear foot is turned out a little, with your heel flat on the floor.

Low stance (*Kiba-dachi* or horse stance)

Stand with your feet wide apart, as if you are sitting on a horse. Keep your body central and low. Keep your back straight. Your knees and feet point slightly inward.

Low backward stance (*Kokutsu-dachi*)

Stand with your rear leg bent and your front leg slightly bent. Turn your rear foot and body sideways, with your head facing to the front. This is a great defensive stance, ready for a counterattack.

Hold your arms and head like this. This is how to **defend** your head, throat and chest.

Keep your chin down.

Hold your left arm up in front of you with fist closed, just below your eyeline.

Hold your right arm so the right fist touches the left elbow.

Always keep knees bent, even if only slightly.

DEFEND!

This stance is called *kokutsu-dachi*. It is a low backward stance, great for defending yourself.

15

Punches

A punch is a strike made using a fist. It is important to make a tight fist so you don't hurt your hand.

Always practice punching with both hands so both sides get strong.

How to make a fist

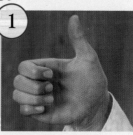

1 Fold your fingertips in tightly toward your hands.

2 Then fold into a fist.

3 Wrap your thumb around the fist. Never put the thumb under your fingers.

The punch

Put both fists together and hold arms straight out in front of you.

Pull the left hand back so it is upside down by your left side.

Punch forward with your left hand while at the same time pulling the right hand back.

Reverse punch

This punch is very effective. Step forward onto your left foot at the same time as you punch with your right fist. The power comes from fist, wrist, elbow, and hips all at once.

TWISTING

When you punch, the punching arm twists to turn the fist so it points down. At the same time the other arm twists so the fist faces up. It takes some practice!

Blocks

*To defend yourself in karate you need to learn how to block an attack. These blocks use your **forearm**, the area betweeen your wrist and your elbow.*

The upper block is usually one of the first blocks taught, and it is one of the simplest to learn.

Upper block

Put your right arm up over your head, and pull your left arm to your side.

Bring your left arm up as you bring your right arm down.

Your arms should be crossing over in front of you.

Snap your left arm upward and pull your right arm back at the same time.

Lower block

(1) Pull your right hand, in a fist, near your left ear.

(2) Snap the right arm down into a block.

(3) Bring your left arm tight to your side, ready to punch if needed.

USING BLOCKS

Sometimes the best attack is a good defense. Blocks can be powerful attacks when done with speed and power. Here a boy is defending against a kick with a powerful lower block.

19

Kicks

A kick is a strike with the foot. Kicks allow you to stay further away from your opponent when you strike. You can kick from the front, back, and side.

Front kick

Start from a left front stance.

Bring right knee up, heel near hips.

Snap leg out into a front kick.

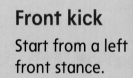

Pull toes back as you push foot out.

Side kick

1

2

3

From an open stance, pull the right foot in toward left knee.

Begin to snap leg out.

Snap leg out and strike with the outside edge of the foot.

Roundhouse kick

1

2

3

Bring right leg up, keeping foot as far behind as possible.

Push your leg out and around.

Fully extend the leg and strike with the ball of the foot.

Strikes

A karate chop is a strike with the side of the hand. It is also called a knife hand. You can also strike with your elbow.

An elbow strike is one of the strongest strikes and can be delivered with power. Elbow strikes are very useful at close range, when your target is too close to make a strong punch.

MONKEY ELBOW

Elbow strikes are called *empi-uchi* in Japanese. "Empi-uchi" means "monkey elbow."

Back elbow strike

1 Look behind you at your target.

2 Cup your left hand over your right hand.

3 Push your right arm back, striking with your elbow.

Karate chop

1 Raise your right hand behind your ear, left hand slightly forward.

2 Snap arm and strike while pulling right arm tight to your waist.

3 Bring right hand around.

Breaking bricks takes years of practice. Don't try it yourself or you may break your hand!

KNIFE HAND

Strike with the bottom edge of your hand, along the red line. Don't hit with your fingers, as it will hurt.

23

How to Improve

You must keep practicing to get better at karate. Keep working on your strikes to build up power. Practice patterns of moves to improve your **technique**.

One way to improve the power of your strike is to train with pads. Take turns holding them with a partner. Build up your speed, strength, and **stamina**.

KIAI!

Try shouting "ee-ya" when you make a strike. It helps you release energy at the right time.

Kata

A *kata* is a series of moves done in a set pattern. They are done without a partner, like training with an imaginary opponent. You can learn every detail of each move this way and practice to get it right.

Kumite

"Kumite" means "fighting." You can practice with a partner, learning to block each other's strikes. Once you are good enough, you can try free fighting.

Kumite **competitors** are usually divided by weight, age, and experience. This makes sure you always fight someone about the same level and size as you. You are free to use any technique, and must be ready to attack and defend at all times.

BUNKAI

If you practice moves with a partner, this is called *bunkai*. You can block each other and practice strikes.

PROTECTION

Gloves, shin and instep protectors, helmets, and mouth guards are worn.

A referee watches the match closely.

Karate Terms

A lot of karate words are in Japanese. The Japanese language uses different symbols to write words. It's fun to learn to recognize some of the symbols.

Empty

Hand

Way

The symbols to the left mean *karatedo*, or "the way of the empty hand." You may see this symbol in your dojo. The symbols are read top to bottom. They are written in **kanji**, a special Japanese script. Japanese has three different alphabets!

CHINA HAND

Originally karate was called "Chinese Hand," not "Empty Hand." The two are said the same but written with different symbols.

One of the times you may hear Japanese at your dojo is when your sensei is counting. He or she may count to keep the rhythm of your punches.

Counting to 10

English	Japanese	Symbol	English	Japanese	Symbol
one	ichi	一	six	roku	六
two	ni	二	seven	shichi (or nana)	七
three	san	三	eight	hachi	八
four	shi (or yon)	四	nine	kyu	九
five	go	五	ten	ju	十

Words you may hear in the dojo

Japanese	How to say it	What it means
arigato gozaimasu	*ah-ree-gah-toh goh-zai-mas*	thank you very much
do itashimas'te	*doh-ee-tash-ee ma-she-tay*	you're welcome
konbon wa	*cone-bon wah*	good evening
konnichi wa	*cone-ichi-ee wah*	good afternoon
rei	*ray*	bow with respect
sensei ni rei	*sen-say nee ray*	bow to the teacher
shomen ni rei	*shoh-men nee ray*	bow to the front
yame	*yah-may*	stop
yoi	*yoy*	ready, attention

In Japanese, each syllable of a word has equal stress.

29

Glossary

combat (KOM-bat)
A fight or contest between individuals or groups.

competitors (kum-PEH-tih-turz)
Those that compete against each other, especially in sports or business.

defend (dih-FEND)
To fight off danger or an attack.

dishonor (dis-ON-er)
A cause of disgrace.

dojo (DOH-joh)
A training center for the martial arts.

forearm (FOR-arm)
The part of the human arm between the elbow and the wrist.

gi (GEE)
A lightweight garment worn for martial arts, usually white loose-fitting pants and a white jacket.

kanji (KAHN-jee)
A Japanese system of writing based on borrowed or modified Chinese characters.

meditate (MEH-dih-tayt)
To spend time in quiet thinking.

opponents (uh-POH-nentz)
A person or thing that opposes another.

sensei (SEN-say)
A teacher or instructor, usually of the Japanese martial arts.

stamina (STA-mih-nuh)
Strength and endurance.

stances (STANS-es)
Ways of standing.

technique (tek-NEEK)
The way in which physical movements are used.

Websites

Due to the changing nature of Internet links, PowerKids Press has developed an online list of websites related to the subject of this book. This site is updated regularly. Please use this link to access the list:
www.powerkidslinks.com/akgma/kara/

Read More

Goodman, Didi. *The Kids' Karate Workbook: A Take-Home Training Guide for Young Martial Artists.* Berkeley, CA: Blue Snake Books, 2009.

Nevius, Carol. *Karate Hour.* Tarrytown, NY: Marshall Cavendish, 2004.

Rielly, Robin L. *Karate for Kids.* Boston, MA: Turtle Publishing, 2004.

Index